LITTLE ANIMAL FRIENDS MAZES

Fran Newman-D'Amico

DOVER PUBLICATIONS, INC.
Mineola, New York

Bibliographical Note

Little Animal Friends Mazes, first published by Dover Publications, Inc., in 2016, is a revised edition of the work originally published by Dover in 2014 as *Animal Friends Mazes.*

International Standard Book Number

ISBN-13: 978-0-486-81035-5
ISBN-10: 0-486-81035-6

Manufactured in the United States by LSC Communications
81035602   2017
www.doverpublications.com

Join familiar animal friends as they wind their way around the sixty fun-filled mazes in this handy-sized activity book. You can help the turkey find his favorite tulips, show the mother bird the way to her baby birds, guide the sheepdog to his bone, and enjoy other similar activities to get the animals on the right path. Use a pencil to draw a line from the Start to the End on each page. When you are finished completing the mazes, you can have even more fun by coloring the pages!

This pig wants to play in the mud, too! Find
the right path for him to take to get there.

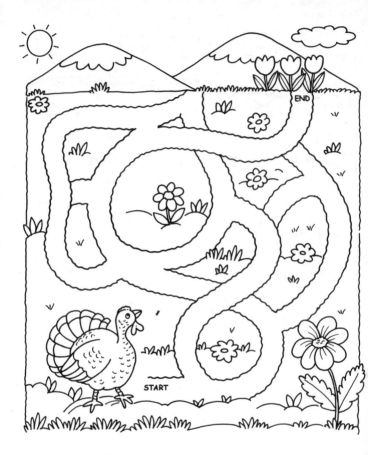

Help the turkey find his favorite tulips.
Show him the way to the end of the path.

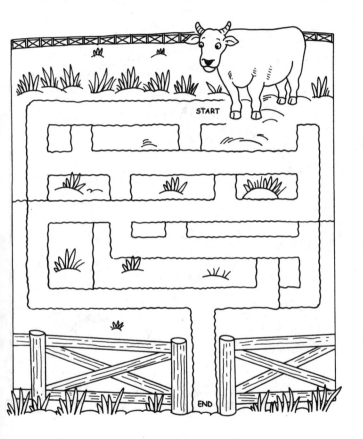

START

END

The ox needs to get to the gate at the end so
that he can go home. Please show him the way.

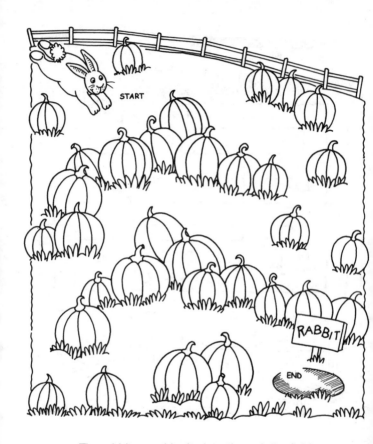

The rabbit goes hippity-hop through the field.
Help her get to the pumpkin patch at the end.

START

END

Find the right path for the goat to take to reach
the other side. Help her get to the end.

END

START

This chicken can't wait to get to her eggs.
Help her find the path to get to them.

START

END

Help the squirrel get to the hole in the
tree trunk to store his acorn.

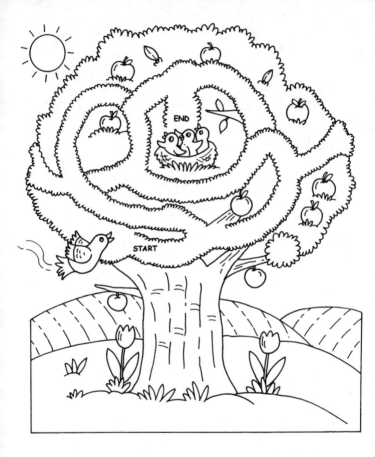

The baby birds are chirping for their mother.
Show her the way to get to the end of the path.

START

END

Horses love to snack on apples. Help this horse follow
the path to reach the basket of tasty apples.

This mouse can smell the cheese in the barn. Please show her the path to take to reach it.

Find the way for the sheep to get to the
shady trees at the end of the path.

The sheepdog buried his bone at the end of the path.
Won't you show him the way to get to the bone?

END

START

The sun's coming up! Help the rooster get to his perch
at the end of the path so he can crow.

The crow would love to sit on top of the scarecrow's head.
Show him the way to get there.

It's time for a swim! Show the duck the way
to the cool pond at the end of the path.

START

END

This cat knows that it's dinnertime. Please show her
the way to get to her food bowl at the end of the path.

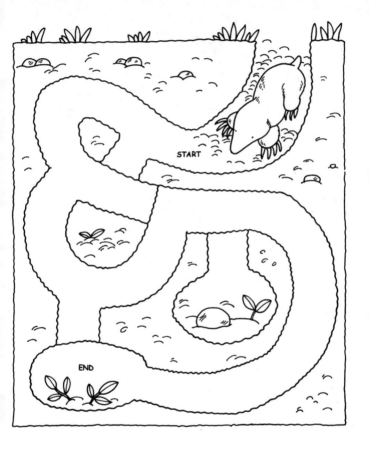

START

END

Moles live in burrows in the ground. Show this mole the way to get to the burrow by following the right path.

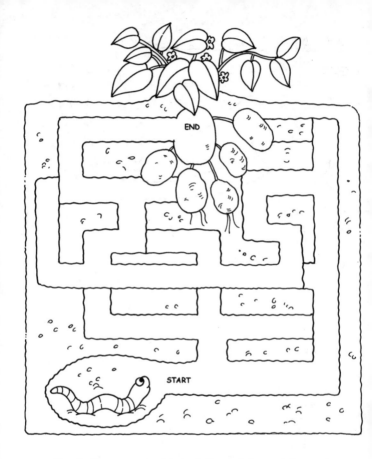

If only the worm could reach the potatoes at the end of the path! You can help by showing the right way.

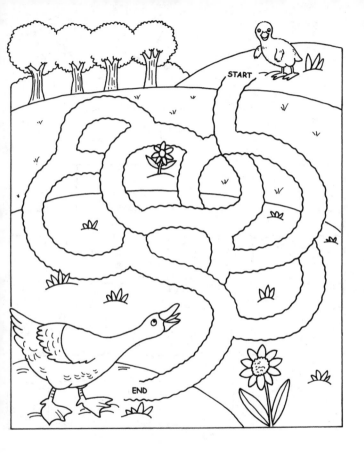

The baby goose has wandered off from his mother. Show him
the way to go to reach her right away!

This spider needs to get back to the web.
Show her the right path to take to get there.

START

END

Please show the right path for the owl
to take to get to her favorite log.

START

END

Buzz! Buzz! Take this busy bee along the right path
to reach the pretty sunflower at the end.

The frog would love to leap along the path to get to the lily pad at the end. Please show the way to get there.

There's a juicy carrot at the end of the path. Show the gopher how to find the way to the carrot.

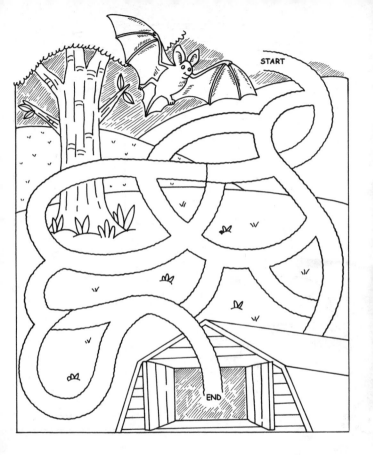

START

END

This bat is ready to go to sleep. Help the bat fly
along to the end of the path and get some rest.

START

END

The ostrich wants to join her baby at the end of the path.
Show her the way to get there.

START

END

The only way for the buffalo to get down to the valley
is to follow the right path. Please show him the way.

START

END

That food at the end of the path looks good to the ram.
Won't you lead him along the path so that he can eat?

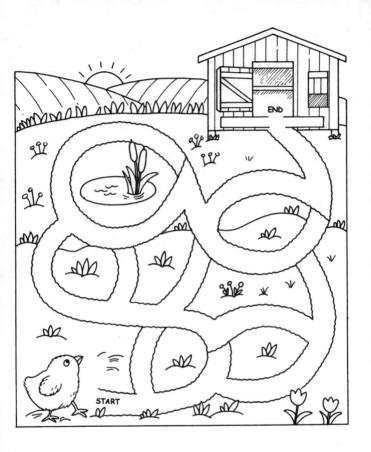

END

START

Oh, no! This chick has lost her way. Please show her
how to get to the chicken coop at the end of the path.

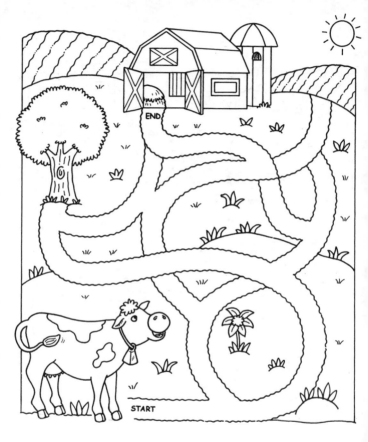

END

START

This cow wants to get back to the barn. She'll be
happy if you show her the way!

END

START

Find the right path and show this prairie dog
the way to his burrow, where he will store his acorn.

START

END

The ostrich needs to get to her egg. You can see
the chick hatching! Please show her the way.

START

END

It's nap time, and the gorilla wants to sleep on
his favorite log. Show him the path to get there.

Koalas eat eucalyptus (you-kuh-lip-tiss) leaves.
Help this koala climb up to get those yummy leaves!

34

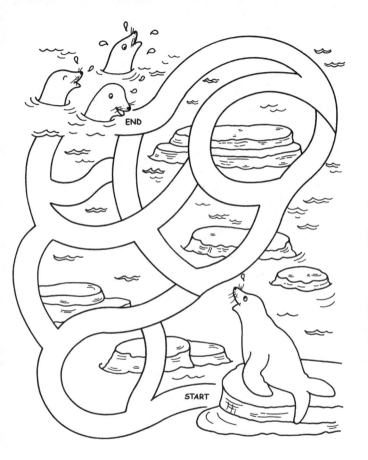

END

START

Seals love to play in the water. Show the seal
at the bottom the way to get to her friends.

The kangaroo and her baby are ready to hop to Kangaroo Hill.
Help them find the way to the end of the trail.

This penguin would like to lie on the rock and enjoy the sun.
Find the path to help him get there.

The elephant is the largest zoo animal. Help this elephant
find the way to the hay at the end of the path.

START

END

A peacock would like to reach the roses at the end of the path.
Help this beautiful bird find the way.

START

END

The lion wants to lie down under that shady tree.
Find the path for him to take to get there.

END

START

Flamingos walk on long, thin legs.
Find the way for this flamingo to get to her friends.

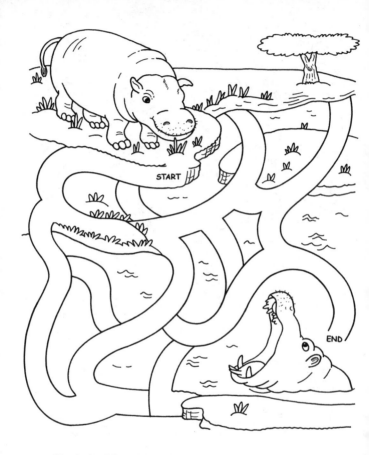

START

END

The baby hippopotamus needs to reach his mother.
Find the path for him to follow to get there.

START

END

A panda chews on bamboo for much of the day.
Help this panda find the way to reach the bamboo forest.

Help this buffalo find the right path to reach
the tasty plants at the end of the trail.

END

START

This sea turtle wants to swim to her friend at the
other end of the stream. Please help her find the way.

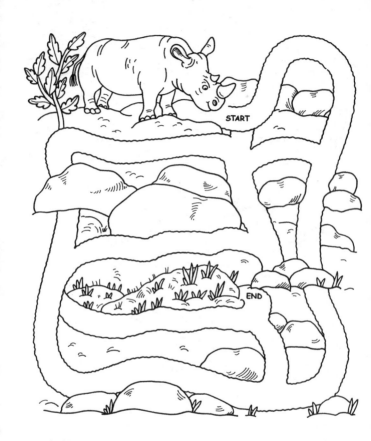

START

END

A rhinoceros is always ready to eat some tender grass.
Help this one find the right path to reach its meal.

END

START

These zebras would like to get back to the trees across the way. Find the path that will take them there.

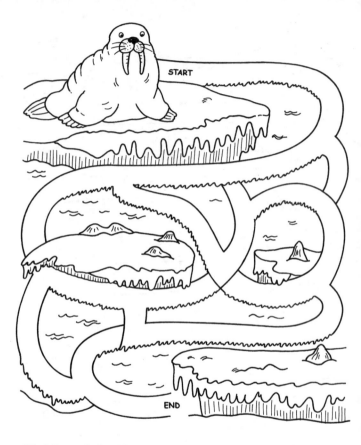

START

END

Find the path for this walrus to take to get to the big iceberg.
He doesn't mind the chilly water!

START

END

This polar bear cub is far from its mother.
Help the mother bear find the path to reach her baby.

END

START

The giraffe at the start of the path wants to join
her friend at the water hole. Please find the way for her.

END

START

A chimpanzee is a good climber.
Help this one find its way to the very top of the tree.

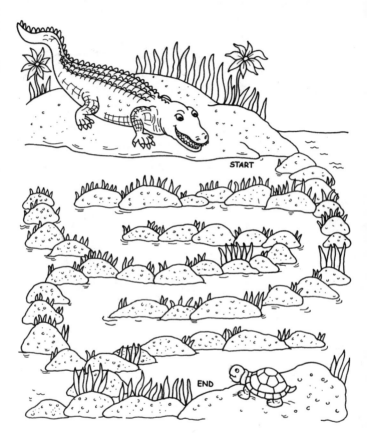

START

END

The alligator wants to visit her turtle friend
on the other side of the swamp. Help her find the path there.

START

END

This tiger needs to get down to the bottom
of the cliff. Find the way for him to get there.

The lemur (lee-mur) on the bottom branch wants to join
her friend up above. Won't you help her find the way?

54

END

START

Show this thirsty camel the way to the water
at the edge of the sand. He will be very grateful.

START

END

The grizzly bear is ready to get some rest in his den.
Find the path for him to follow to reach it.

The otters are waiting for their friend
to join them in the stream. Please show her the way.

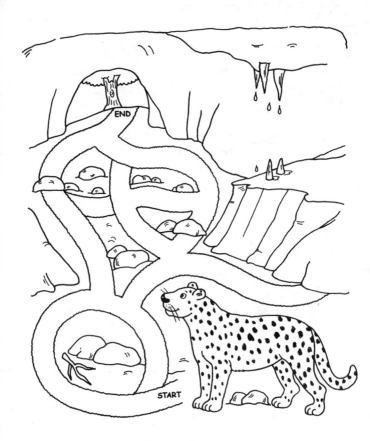

END

START

This leopard has to follow a winding path to leave his cave.
Show him the way to go outside.

It's a long way for the snake to reach her home.
Show her the path to take around the cactus to get there.

Llamas are great climbers. Help this one find her way to the flat top of the mountain.

60